HOW GOD CAN SAVE YOU
FROM ADDICTION

How God Can Save You From Addiction

PETER BARSKI

Lone Wolf Publishing

Contents

I   1

Chapter 1

How God Can Save You
From Addiction
by Peter Barski

Intro

If one person can find Hope from reading this story, then I have accomplished what I set out to do. I give God all the glory for this book, the events that led me to this point in my life, His grace and mercy, and the time and resources allotted to me to relay this message. This book is meant for lifting that one person out of the depths of despair; to encourage that one soul, no matter how far they have fallen from grace, and give them Hope. It does not matter if that person is a former millionaire who has lost all their wealth due to a severe drug addiction, or a person in jail, facing a life of uncertainty, with no one or nowhere to turn. In effect, you have but one choice to make, and that is to turn to God and trust Him for deliverance, or to try to crawl out of that deep, dark hole you found yourself in on your own accord.

But life was meant to be lived in fellowship with God, with closeness to Him, entrusting Him with our lives. He is there, waiting for you to turn to Him and ask for help. Will you make that choice right now? Think of where you are right now. Has living a life apart from God really been that fulfilling? Are you possibly contemplating suicide? Are you in a jail cell with no one to turn to for help? I have been there myself my friend, and it is not a pleasant place to be. It is because of my experiences in these matters that I felt compelled to share my story of hope, even for the poor soul who has hit rock bottom.

"Ah," but you say, "I am facing years of prison time for the crimes I have committed, there is no hope for me!" So too was I; seventeen years to be exact for the two felonies I was charged with. I was all alone to face a seemingly endless abyss of trouble that lay before me. But God loves the brokenhearted and He has mercy for the humble, and when I cried out to Him to save me, He delivered me! And so it is with great joy that I share this news with you. God had a plan for me, one I could not see back then, but one I can clearly see now, which is to share this message of hope and joy to those who are suffering.

Please come with me on a journey of deliverance and find hope in this story. Make the right decision and turn to God for help, for with God anything is possible. I am a living testimony to this fact. Thank you God for these words of encouragement and for Your countless blessings!

My Past

Addiction can start off subtly, but it eventually spirals downward into an avalanche of trouble. It was all around me growing up, though I did not truly recognize it until later on in my life. My father had been what they call a "functioning alcoholic," starting a successful real estate company and later an appraisal business, while my mother would drink hard liquored cocktails until passing out after dinner. We were a middle class family that on the surface seemed as normal as any other, but underneath my parents were unhappy together. This would become more apparent towards the end of their marriage. My younger sibling and I would pick up on their unhappiness, subconsciously I believe, causing us to react in different ways. My sibling would spend hours alone in her bedroom, becoming reclusive, while I dabbled in marijuana use. Though not addressed amongst us, our parent's unhappiness permeated into our mental mindset. My sibling became somewhat of a recluse, never marrying or having children, and my drug use would eventually evolve into a full blown addiction.

After their divorce, my father and I stayed in the house we grew up in, while my mother and sibling settled down with her family further south. I soon joined the Navy and became a pharmacy technician. I was always drawn towards the medical profession, but was too queasy around blood, so I went into the field of pharmacy. I spent almost seven years in the service, working in two clinics. During that time I got married and had one son, but being young, the relationship quickly ended in a divorce.

Wanting more in life, I decided to go to college. I enrolled full time in a junior college with the hopes of eventually going to pharmacy school. I excelled in the majority of my classes, having found a renewed desire to learn after spending some time away from school. During this time my sibling had finished law school and was clerking for the government up in Washington DC.

After three years I earned my Associate's degree and got accepted into two pharmacy programs. I chose the one closer to my parents, both of whom were now residing in Broward County. It was 1996 and it felt like I had my whole life ahead of me. Despite his daily drinking, my father was able to start a successful appraisal business, even hiring a second person to help out. My mother worked for her youngest sister as a nanny and never remarried. Things seemed to be heading in the right direction.

But upon entering pharmacy school, I joined a fraternity, which in and of itself wasn't a bad thing, but it did expose me to lots of drinking and partying. I soon found myself dabbling in marijuana use again, which affected my priorities. I studied less and pursued women more, sometimes staying out past two in the morning, even on school nights. I was having what

I thought was the time of my life, and though my grades suffered, I was always able to squeak out a passing grade at the end of each grading term. But despite all the pleasures and fun times I was exposed to, I felt an emptiness that I could not explain. Regret for my sexual encounters I had the night before was only pacified by more drinking and partying the next night. This only ended once our classes finished and our clinical rotations began. This period of time was meant to expose us to the different aspects of pharmacy and help us chose which niche we would want to practice once we graduated. But for me I began dating coworkers I came across, ignoring the rules of boundaries. One could argue that it is natural for a young man to "sow his wild oats," but it isn't what God wants for us, which is why I had such an empty feeling inside of me, one that could not be quenched by romantic encounters.

And so even though I curtailed my drinking and drug use, I substituted it with promiscuity. It was a trait I carried forward in my life for some time, always seeking a sort of self gratification that really didn't satisfy me, though it provided me with a sort of short-term pleasure. This substituting one addiction for another, coupled with bad judgment, would later cost my freedom.

I eventually finished rotations and passed the state licensing exam, becoming a full fledged pharmacist. I started working at a large grocery store chain and was soon able to purchase a home. Life seemed to be well for me; I was financial secure and working a stable job. I met who would become my second wife at the store I worked in. She was an office manager who worked evenings and would come to the pharmacy at night to retrieve the till. Things progressed quickly and it wasn't long before she gave birth to our daughter. For the next few years things proceeded somewhat normally and we were very happy. But life can throw you a curve ball at times, catching you off guard, and in my case leading me down to a new level of addiction and pain.

The Fall

The summer of 2004 was a dark time for me. The health of both of my parents declined rapidly; my mother battling congestive heart failure and my father contending with Parkinson's disease. That was also the year we had back to back hurricanes within a month of each other along the Florida eastern coast. It was a stressful time indeed.

After Hurricane Frances came through, my mother passed away from her condition. She had been dealing with depression and alcoholism for some time, and those things coupled with her heart failure proved to be too much. She was only 64 years old. Meanwhile my father's tremors and shaking had gotten so bad he could not go anywhere alone. He required assistance just to get out the door of his condo. Then Hurricane Jeanne came through, knocking out the power in our area for an extended period of time and flooding the coastal region. It was hot and humid and many people's homes and belongings were damaged. Debris lined the highways for often miles long stretches. It was a real mess.

Then one morning I got a call from my sibling that dad had passed away. He had fallen while getting out of bed and hit his head on a dresser. I remember cursing God's name and throwing my cell phone down to the ground in anger and frustration. All these events happened within just a month's time or so, almost too much for me to bear mentally.

Then one afternoon while trying to fix a leak on the roof, I herniated a disk in my lower back while trying to lift a bucket of tar. The pain was excruciating. I had to miss several days of work and immediately sought medical advice. The first specialist I saw wanted to perform some elaborate surgery, cutting me open from the front, moving my intestines aside and then replacing my herniated disk with a prosthetic one of some sort. You can imagine the fear that beset me picturing all of that in my mind, not to mention that I was only in my thirties, way too young to have to go through that kind of surgery.

Then someone suggested I go see a pain management doctor. Despite being a pharmacist, it seemed like a novel idea. "What a simple solution to a complicated issue," I thought. I had all the items needed to become a legitimate patient: referrals, x-rays and even an MRI. And so began my decent into the world of opiates. I was promptly put on Vicodin and Xanax, the later used to help "relax my back muscles." Then after only a few months, Oxycontin was added to my regimen. I remember to this day how I felt after taking the first pill. I was at the movies and took one just before going into the theater. Now some people will tell you that they get nauseas or sick after taking a pain pill, or they fall asleep, but not an addict. Within fifteen minutes or so I felt a relaxing calmness overtake me. With each beat of my heart it left like a soothing warmness pumped through my veins. It was unlike anything I had experienced before.

I do not want to glorify the feeling opiates give a person, for this initial feeling is seldom felt again by a user. It is what is called "chasing the dragon," in that the user takes more and more of the drug, trying to experience that same initial sensation they had, but never seemingly able to find it. In the process they forgo health and basic needs, lose relationships and may even end up in jail or worse. The pursuit of that initial "high" takes priority over all things, which then leads to them just having to score some of the drug in order not to get sick and experience withdrawals. It's a vicious cycle that can ultimately lead to one's overdose if help isn't sought.

As time went on, my usage escalated. I found a doctor in south Florida who would prescribe me over two hundred oxy-codone 30mg tablets and ninety 15mg oxycodone tablets each month. Whenever I would find myself running low, I had the means to order additional drugs online, since I was still working at the time. I found myself becoming more depressed and antisocial. Work became too demanding for me and my wife became unhappy with our relationship, which began to crumble. By the year 2013 I had quit my job and my wife moved in with her mother. It was now just my son and I living together in the home, and though my spouse was less than ten miles away, it might as well have been another continent. That is how far we had emotionally drifted apart from each other, but as I would soon see, the worst was yet to come.

Crashed But Not Burned

By April of 2014 I had completely run out of money and was not sure how I was going to pay for food. That is how far down I had travelled with my addiction. I was tired and lonely and just wanted to get my life back in order. It was then that I decided to quit taking drugs altogether, "cold turkey." It was a poor decision, as being on potent opiates for ten years, not to mention Xanax as well, I should have sought professional help. But being a healthcare professional myself, I thought I had things completely under control. What a disaster that decision turned out to be!

It turns out that being on high doses of opiates for so long and then suddenly stopping can be most uncomfortable, as anyone who has tried will tell you. And though it usually is not fatal for a person to, stopping opiates cold turkey will most certainly make you wish you were not alive. But what can be fatal is stopping Xanax, which is a benzodiazepine, cold turkey. Doing so can cause fatal seizures and one should always seek professional treatment if they are on such a medicine and wish to stop taking it. Fortunately for me, I did not have a fatal seizure, but I did end up suffering a mental breakdown that led me to being placed in a psychiatric facility for two days.

You see, when a person abruptly stops taking the kind of drugs I was on, their body goes through anhedonia. Rather than try to define what that is, let me tell you what happened to me and explain the symptoms I developed. Within a day I became nauseous and lightheaded. After the second day I developed diarrhea and lost all appetite for food. At night I felt hot and sweated profusely, while during the day I was shivering cold and wrapped myself up in blankets. I could not sleep even though I was exhausted and eventually I began to lose weight and develop tremors. My electrolytes became imbalanced and after a month of these persistent symptoms, I became paranoid and delirious. I began to hear voices and listened to conversations that did not exist. Most of these "conversations" were of people I had known that were talking about me, and I became even more paranoid.

I began to contemplate suicide and thought of ways to accomplish it. One day I imagined myself cut my wrists while lying in bed, though it almost seemed real to me, as if I were watching myself do it. Needless to say, I was in really bad shape, physically and emotionally.

Finally on Mother's Day in 2014, my son, concerned about my welfare, went to a neighbor's house and the police were called. I was admitted to a psychiatric facility by ambulance and much of the next few days were a blur to me. I do know that I spent most of that time sleeping. I literally gave up on life and just relinquished myself to fate, it was all I could do.

Upon hearing what happened, my father-in-law, who was a Vietnam veteran, took pity on me and let me move in with him and his wife. He had a spare bedroom where I could sleep, and sleep I did! He also got me enrolled into the VA system since I was a veteran as well. I would like to take this moment and urge any veteran out there who may be reading this and is struggling with drug addiction to please seek help at any nearby VA hospital or clinic. They will never turn down a veteran in need of help and they provide excellent service. I saw an addiction psychiatrist, who put me on a proper treatment to manage my Xanax withdrawals.

My health began to improve slowly, and though I was utterly embarrassed by the whole incident, I was blessed to have someone take me into their home and provide for me. My father-in-law was a patient and gracious man, and there was no judgment passed. I felt accepted and there were no probing questions about how I had let myself get into such a situation. In his house we only looked ahead and moved forward. I cannot say enough for how good he and his wife were to me. I was very fortunate.

Substituting

Once my physical and mental health was restored, my father-in-law turned toward the daunting task of my financial ruin. My truck had been repossessed and my home was in danger of being foreclosed on. Arrangements were made to sell the house and the money that we made from its sale was used to pay off my wife's care and my truck. I did not think that I would be able to practice my profession again, but he encouraged me to try. So I began the arduous task of job searching, and to my delight found a job for a pharmacy technician in a small, independent pharmacy. Though it was not a pharmacist position, and the pay was much less than what I had been making, I was just happy to be working in the environment I was trained in.

I soon found out that the pharmacist I now worked alongside of was in recovery. He had struggled with prescription drugs also and was now over ten years sober. He introduced me to Alcoholics Anonymous (AA) and we shared our stories with each other. I found it very encouraging that there was another pharmacist who had past problems with opiates and yet was now in recovery and back to practicing again. There was hope for me yet!

But then the Department of Health (DOH) contacted me. Someone had typed an anonymous letter to them informing them that I had addiction issues and was now seeking employment as a pharmacist. They were voicing their concern for welfare of the "public's safety." Only a few people knew I was seeking employment and even fewer still knew of my addiction issues, so I could make a fair guess as to who had sent it, but that is irrelevant now. Because of the letter, an investigation began and I was referred to a professional monitoring program. After an evaluation, it was recommended I attend an inpatient rehab for three months, even though I had been sober for several months. I would also be subject to random drug tests for the next five years and see a therapist weekly. If I did not comply, I would have to give up my license to practice. In my father-in-law's words, "what choice did I have?"

So I begrudgingly went to a rehab facility that specialized in seeing healthcare professionals. Though I was unhappy with this turn of events, I did learn a lot about recovery. I was actually shocked at the number of other healthcare workers who were there as patients. I met other pharmacists, a nurse anesthetist, a cardiac surgeon, a couple of plastic surgeons and even a psychiatrist. They all had their "demons" they were battling, from alcohol to opiates and even amphetamines. But no matter what I learned in rehab, I was still destined to fail in my recovery because I was lacking one thing, and that was God.

After completing rehab, I went to stay with my father-in-law again, but only for a short period of time. I quickly found a job as a full-time pharmacist, and I rented a house closer to where I was working. Though clean and sober, I began to substitute drugs with women, despite still being married. I joined several dating apps and began seeing various women for usually short lived encounters. Not long after, my wife wanted a divorce, and we mutually filed with the court without involving any lawyers. It was a selfish period for me that I was oblivious to at the time, but is easy to see now.

Instead of taking time to contemplate the demise of my marriage, I continued on the dating apps. Then the unthinkable happened, I fell in love. She was a nurse who understood recovery because her father had been an alcoholic and was now sober. Even though she was still married, it didn't matter to me. She was in the midst of getting a divorce and that was excuse enough for me to justify our relationship. But as with any relationship lacking a strong spiritual foundation, it was destined to failure. We started a cycle of breaking up, seeing other people and then getting back together. It was an unhealthy alliance, and after two years of it, she ended things between us. I was devastated. I had never really experienced that level of passion with someone before, and though we would often argue, I was in love with her. Unfortunately I was also selfish and hurtful, and it ultimately cost me the relationship. I became emotionally distraught and a thick fog of depression set in on me, but the worse was still yet to come.

Hitting Rock Bottom

I was very unhappy at this point and desperate to replace the relationship I had just lost. Instead of taking time to heal and learn from the mistakes I made, I wanted to just jump right into something else to help alleviate the mental pain I was experiencing. Then one afternoon while at work, I noticed a beautiful woman come into the pharmacy. The fact that she was purchasing insulin syringes did not deter me from going down and taking to her. We exchanged phone numbers and not soon after began seeing each other physically. She was an active drug user, which should have been a "red flag" for me since I was in recovery. But I ignored that fact as I was so infatuated with her. It didn't take long for her to ask for money to help support her drug addiction, which I freely gave to her just to make her happy.

Her IV drug habit cost anywhere from $120 to $200 a day. Although I was a pharmacist and made good money, it didn't take long for me to max out my credit cards. Then she began dropping subtle suggestions taking pills from my workplace. Being around her injecting drugs prompted me to start take pain medicine again, which quickly affected my good judgment. As money became scarce and we became more desperate, I truly began to contemplate stealing from the pharmacy.

It would turn out to be a "fool's errand" as my employer was already keeping a close eye on me and his controlled drug inventory. There was talk amongst the pharmacy staff of my dating an addict, and this was not taken lightly there. In any case, I agreed to take one bottle of sixty pills of her drug of choice, to help us out "just this one time." She promised me we would get ourselves "straightened out" and this would give us the "breathing room" we needed to do so.

So on a Saturday when at work, I took a bottle, feeling very uneasy doing so. The guilt was weighing heavily on me and I just had a bad feeling I would get caught. Sure enough, later on in the week I was arrested by two DEA agents and charged with larceny and trafficking, both felony counts. Booked into the county jail, I told the guards I was suicidal, so I was placed on suicide watch. By doing so I was not allowed any clothes except for a black foam vest that barely covered me and then placed into a single cell with no bedding or bunk. All I could do was either stand or sit on the cement floor. That night a guard slid a plastic mat into my cell for me to sleep on. For two days I remained in that cell with no access to a phone and my bond set at $75,000. I had truly hit my rock bottom. It was then that I prayed to Jesus to forgive me of all my sins and to save me from my dire straits.

Glimmers Of Hope

"If you are walking in darkness, without a ray of light, trust in the Lord and rely on your God." Isaiah 50:10

After two days I was asked by the medical staff if I was still suicidal. I promptly responded "No!" and explained why I had said what I did; wanting to not around other inmates. Due to protocol, I was not put in with the general population, but rater in the psych unit of the jail. I was told that after a week there I could be brought over to the general population. But it was a step up from where I had been. I now had a bunk bed to sleep on, and though I had a roommate, it was a welcome sight to not have to sleep on the concrete floor. I was also allowed to dress in orange jail clothing which obviously covered much more of my body.

The next day I was given access to a phone and reached out to my sister for help. Being a lawyer in Florida, I thought she could at least find me another attorney who could help me make bail and get me out of jail quickly. But to my complete dismay, she stopped taking my phone calls after our first conversation and by the end of that day had changed her number altogether. It was a "wake up call" I will never forget. I literally had no other family I could turn to for help. It seemed as if I had nowhere to turn and was facing a long period of time there. If you have even been arrested then you can relate that the first priority for you is to get released, no matter what you are charged with. And so it was with me, but it seemed like a dauntless task.

Just when I thought all was hopeless, I found out from an inmate that I could call any local bail company directly without having to call collect. In fact, there was a list of them next to the one phone in our jail wing. It may sound like common knowledge to someone who has been arrested before, but since that was not my case, I was just becoming aware of that fact. Since time outside your jail cell is limited, I had to anxiously wait before I called the first bail bondsman that was recommended to me. She was able to pull my arrest information up on her computer, and since my bail had been set at $75,000,

I needed to come up with $7,500, or ten percent in order to get out. This was another thing I was not aware of, in order to bail out of jail, you or someone you know who is willing to pay must come up with the ten percent before a bail bondsman will submit the required papers for your release. I began to wonder if that was why my sister had stopped taking my calls, fearing I would ask her for money.

Fortunately for me I had a stock account that had about $10,000 in it. Once they were able to verify that, they arranged for my release, and by evening time I was out. I will never take my freedom for granted again, that is for sure. It is something that many people take for granted.

Once I was out, I still continued to see the woman with whom I had gotten into so much trouble with. There was no more talk of taking medicine from my workplace as I was now unemployed and basically unhirable given my two pending felony charges. It wasn't until I was completely broke that she ended thing between us. That is a characteristic trait of addicts: to use people for their own benefit for as long as they can, then move on to doing the same thing to someone else in order to feed their habit. Lesson learned.

I was now left with much time on my hands, and to make the most of it, I decided to read the entire Bible, starting with the book of Genesis. I had already read much of the New Testament and some sporadic parts of the Old Testament, but I never really seemed to have time to just sit down and slowly read the entire thing straight through. This I believe is the start to building a proper relationship with God. It helps you to understand why Jesus had to come into the world; to become the perfect sacrifice so that we can pray to Him to forgive our sins and be made acceptable to God. Only then can we receive the true blessings from God that we need. And that is what I did, I earnestly prayed for Jesus to forgive me of all my sins, past and present, and to help me in my dire situation. I can tell you that after doing so, I felt a certain calmness fall upon me, despite that fact that I was facing almost two decades in prison. I was able to let go of all anxieties and fears surrounding my future, knowing that God was in control. What a beautiful feeling it was.

By reading the Bible completely I was able to learn about the people God chose to use. And not just individuals, but the people of Israel as a whole also. Many of them did bad things, but when they confessed and repented, trusting God to save them, their lives were restored. That is the beautiful thing about God's love, it is without measure and there for you to receive, if you only ask. Jesus said that He came not to judge the world, but to save it, and that God so loved the world that He sent His only begotten son to die for us, so that we may be saved. It is the humbled, imprisoned, the downtrodden and oppressed that God loves. Do not think that your past sins and crimes have made you too unacceptable to God. Don't feel that you have done or seen things that have rendered you a "lost soul." Nothing could be farther from the truth. God wants to restore you to Him if you but just ask.

Take King David in the Bible. He was described as a man after God's own heart, and yet David had slept with a married woman, getting her pregnant in the process. David then ordered his army commander to put Bathsheba's husband out into the front line of battle, then retreat suddenly, leaving him to be killed in action. Essentially David arranged for his murder. In just a short period of time David had coveted his neighbor's wife, committed adultery with her and then had her husband murdered so that he could have her all to himself. Hardly the actions of a righteous man, and yet realizing his sins, David earnestly prayed to God for forgiveness, and found favor in God's eyes. His sin did not go without consequence in that the baby died, and that is the lesson to be learned from his story. We all are not perfect and have committed many sins, sins with their consequences, but if we decide to pray for forgiveness and turn away from the things that cause us to sin, God will restore us to Himself, and the blessings that can come from that are truly amazing! David eventually had another child with Bathsheba, Solomon, who would later become renowned for his wisdom and for building a magnificent temple for God.

You may be facing a long prison sentence or are homeless due to an addiction and a life apart from God, but it is never too late to ask for forgiveness and ask God for help! Of course our sinful actions have consequences, and we all have to face them, but wouldn't it be better to face them with God on our side, and not alone? Please give it a try dear reader, you will be surprised by just how far God can pull you out of your present circumstances. I was to be sure. When I look back at where I was and where I am now, I can't help but praise God for all He has done for me, as you will soon read. Thank you God!

A Reprieve

"Whenever we forget how we are bound together in God,
we do damage to ourselves and others." Winn Collier

Since my financial situation was bleak at best, I was appointed a public defender. Given the charges, most people would have considered my situation dire at best, and not being able to afford a private attorney only seemed to darken that outlook. But in a divine turn of events, I was offered the opportunity to move my case to drug court, where if I would complete the one year program, the charges, both of them, would be dropped. The program was not without its challenges to be sure. I was subject to random drug testing seven days a week, required to find a job and also to attend weekly group sessions and monthly therapy with a drug addiction specialist. But in comparison to the possible seventeen year prison sentence, I immediately agreed to the offer. It was an opportunity I feel brought on by the grace of God.

About six months into the program the COVID-19 pandemic hit, and the country was essentially shut down. I used the stimulus checks given to me to keep up with my mortgage payments and found an agency that paid my utility bill as long as I remained in good standing with the program. I found a job as a telemarketer, selling fruit baskets, and for a while even drove a tow truck. I did what was required of me and was thankful for my freedom.

As I read through the Bible, my faith grew tremendously. I was able to see God's handiwork in my life and all of His blessings. I learned that the Old Testament pointed to Jesus and His coming to earth from Heaven. I was also able to see just how much God loved us and longed for our reliance on Him. I was able to see that God could and can make anything happen, even the impossible, if we would just trust Him completely.

Trusting God completely was for me the hardest thing to do. All of our lives we are taught not to trust others; that the only one we can trust is ourselves. "If you want something done right, do it yourself," is the standard taught by many parents. Perhaps when relating to people that is the case, but when it comes to God, we should trust Him and rely on Him completely, abandoning our instinct to "go it alone." What has life without God accomplished for me or you? Addiction, depression, or anxiety? Homelessness or imprisonment? But this standard taught to us throughout our lives of not trusting others is a hard trait to let go of. It goes against the very grain of society these days. But to let go and let God, so to speak, is the only way we can live a life free from addiction and fear. To become totally reliant on Him for our needs and our wants is what I feel is our purpose. To continue to go it alone in this world will only produce disappointment in the long run.

This is the start of living a life free of addiction. Understanding that God wants what is best for us is key and the first step to spiritual and physical recovery. To know that He loves us beyond measure is sadly never learned by some people. They turn to others for acceptance or love, and when disappointed, often turn to using drugs instead. But God never lets down those who seek him faithfully. In fact God is referred to as a father in the Bible, our spiritual Father, and we are His children. What child is not totally reliant on their parents to provide for them? To provide a home and food to eat is not a basic right so much as it is instinct. Even though there are earthly parents who neglect their children, God is perfect and pure in every way. He would never leave us starving or without shelter if we but turn our hearts and our souls over to Him in complete abandonment. And so to trust God to deliver us from our situation, whatever that may be, is the first step to our recovery here on earth.

By trusting God with my circumstances, I was able to successfully complete drug court and also not lose my home. God spared me a lengthy prison sentence and so, so much more. It was by letting go of my self reliance and trusting God to provide for me that I was able to accomplish all of that. Have you tried relying on other people or yourself and come up short? Isn't it time to trust your heavenly Father, the One who truly loves you and wants to provide for you? All you have to do is ask. Ask Jesus to forgive you of all your past sins, and for God to deliver you of your drug habit. To make it possible to overcome that addiction and all the troubles that comes with it.

Closing Ranks

"Great are the works of the Lord; they are pondered by all who delight in them." Psalm 111:2

Closing ranks is a military term used to describe when a group of soldiers form straight lines and group together in flanks. They narrow the space between themselves and the soldier next to them. It produces and orderly appearance to a large rank of individuals. It is also a term used by a good friend of mine that describes when a person chooses to not come in contact with individuals who are sinful or toxic in nature. By doing so it will have the effect of reducing the number of people in that individual's inner circle, so to speak. This helps to produce a more stable and peaceful environment for that person. It also helps with their walk with God in my opinion.

By not associating with a fellow addict, it helps to keep that temptation to use again to a minimum. Especially someone who is contemplating quitting drugs or just out of rehab, it minimizes that risk of us using again. By blocking our drug dealer's phone number so that they cannot call us to see if we need anything, that helps us in our recovery. By avoiding the street on which you know that dealer works on, you avoid that chance of running into them. By deleting our friends on social media who might contact you on that platform to ask if you have any drugs they could buy, it closes that circle of "friends" that may cause you to relapse. You see my point, it is the narrowing of bad influences that helps you on your road of recovery and keeps you focused on staying clean. Though no person is perfect, we are intelligent enough to know what can cause us to relapse, and thereby intelligent enough to avoid those people and things.

Jesus tells us that "if our right eye causes us to sin, then gouge it out. It is better to enter Heaven with one eye than to perish in death with both eyes." Does He mean that literally? Of course not, but if you find yourself going to a friend's house that you know uses drugs, then you are only leading yourself to temptation. It would be better for you to lose that friend than to continue to relapse. Is it really so necessary for you to keep seeing that person, or keeping that dealer's number programmed in your phone? Using drugs is not what God intended for you, and it only serves to separate yourself from Him.

Sometimes it takes having to hit rock bottom for a person to finally cut out of their lives the things that causes them to use drugs. Try to think of that as God getting your attention. Wouldn't you rather be dope sick for a while than continually living a life without God? But you would be surprised how He can pull you through the difficult times if you but seek and ask Him for help. People will offer you help that you would had never had suspected to. Things will become possible through avenues that you never thought of. It is just taking that first step to earnestly pray for help that will open the door. All you have to do is ask. It really is that simple.

In all honesty, using drugs only serves to separate us from God. We were meant for so much more in this life. A life filled with God's blessings, and it can start by making that choice to stop using. Let God take it from there and you will be surprised by what He can accomplish in your life.

"Easier said than done," one might argue. "If I just stop injecting 'fetty' I will get sick." But ask yourself a question: what are you doing to support your habit? Are you stealing from someone or prostituting yourself? If you land in jail, the guards will have no sympathy on you, and you will end up sick in a much worse off place. Is it a chance you want to take? Trust me when I tell you, there are far better places that can manage your withdrawals than a jail cell. Ask for help from a relative, friend or even a healthcare professional. Just be honest with them and ask for help before it is too late.

As time went on, I removed the things that caused me to sin or distracted me from God. I took time for myself and became comfortable being alone. I no longer sought the company of meaningless relationships or toxic people. It was as if I could breathe again, being comfortable in my own skin. I stopped going onto dating apps and stopped seeking prostitutes online. I even stopped watching so much television, finding everything boring or trivial compared to God's Word. I used to plan my days around what shows to watch, but reading and learning from the Bible became paramount for me. I began to watch the sunsets from my front porch, listening to the birds chirp, giving thanks to God for I had. I put down my phone and looked around me more, becoming thankful for my home and family. When driving to work I would turn off the radio and look at the beautiful sunrises. I gave thanks to God for the car I had that took me to work and was even thankful to be working. I made God my priority and saw the changes He was making in my life, which made me thankful for all I had, and made it clearer to me all that He accomplished for me. Seek God and be amazed by what He can do for you.

The God of all Comfort

"Come to Me, all of you who are weary and carry heavy burdens, and I will give you rest." Matthew 11:28

One day while travelling to the beach and not in any particular hurry, I saw a rack of books in front of a consignment shop with a sign "free books" above them. So I pulled in and looked through the selection they had. One book in particular stood out to me, "The God of all Comfort" by Hannah Whitall Smith. It turned out to be the best book I've ever read that explains the character of God. I recommend it to anyone who wants to understand God better. It is not a substitute to the Bible, but read in conjunction with, it is an amazing counterpart to it. Especially for someone wanting to grow closer to God and understand what He wants for us, it is a good read. The title of the book sums it up nicely, which is that God is the God of all comfort.

What does that mean exactly? Well it doesn't mean that we will live a life here on earth without any challenges. But when we trust God completely, our anxieties disappear. Our worries fade like fog in the early morning sun. By putting our trust in God and letting Him take care of us that this is accomplished. This seems to go against out nature somewhat as all of our lives we are taught to trust no one. "If you want something done right, do it yourself," is the motto engraved into us. But

God is our Heavenly Father, and He delights in our reliance on Him. All things good come from God if we only ask.

The book also explains how God is a loving Father who cares for us as His own children. We all know good earthly fathers, or can at least imagine one. A good father would feed his children when they are hungry and provide shelter for them, clothes and more. Now imagine how much more so our Heavenly Father wants to provide for us, a Father who created us and loves us beyond measure. There is no need to doubt that He will provide what's best for you, if you only ask. When you were young, was there ever a doubt that your parents would provide for you, that is if they were good, loving parents? That is how we should feel about God and all He provides us with. It should become second nature to us.

But you may ask, "If my Heavenly Father loves me so much, then why am I in this jail cell right now?" You should be asking, "What was it I did that got me here?" Like our earthly fathers who scolded or corrected us for our wrong doings as kids, so God does to us as well. There are always consequences to our sins, but it is never too late to confess them to Jesus and turn to God for guidance. Sometimes it takes a person to hit rock bottom before they cry out to God for help. How much better it is to depend on Him before we reach that rock bottom! It is God's way perhaps of getting our attention. We only need to turn away from our sinful ways: using drugs, prostituting ourselves, ect and turn to God. Stop being so self reliant and start trusting your Heavenly Father from whom all good things come. Nothing pleases Him more than our utter dependence on Him for all our earthly needs.

So what is the first step? It is to confess our sins to Jesus and ask Him to forgive us for all our wrong doings, making us acceptable to God. Isn't it time you took that first step and got right with God? Have all your friends or family turned away and left you with no one to turn to? Do you feel like you have hit such a low that you just don't see any way out? Perhaps this is your time to sincerely ask for God's help and see what happens. Perhaps it is time to turn your life around with the Grace of God.

God's Timing

This is the confidence we have in approaching God: that if we ask anything according to His will, He hears us." 1 John 5:14

An addict is a "here and now" type of individual, as any former addict will tell you. Having to score the next fix as quickly as possible to prevent getting dope sick becomes a way of life, no matter what that entailed. It creates in that person a sense of constant urgency all the time. Addicts will prostitute themselves, steal from others and spend every last dollar they have in order to get their next fix. Their life is in a perpetual hurry fueled by their need for the next score, always in a hurry. This type of personality trait carries over many times once they quit. In recovery it may be hard to shake that "here and now" mentality. I experienced this characteristic long after I was released from jail. It took me a long time to see this in myself and to trust in God's timing, but once I did so completely, it utterly felt as though I shed all anxieties. It is an amazing feeling to be sure.

Of course being in prison or jail, one is most certainly occupied with getting out, as quickly as possible. But acceptance is key. Accepting responsibility for what you did to get you there is the next step in your walk with God. Claiming that you don't belong where you are now is not taking responsibility for your actions. Sin is not without its consequences, and you can not fool God. Feeling sorry for yourself won't help either, it will only cause depression. I had accepted my fate while in the back of the patrol car taking me off to jail. There was no denying what I had done to get me in that predicament. But it does not mean you can't ask God for help.

Being patient and trusting God to deliver you from whatever circumstance you are facing is important. You have to shed that here and now mentality and fully trust in God's timing. It may not happen in the time frame you desire, but knowing God is at work and in your corner helps to alleviate anxieties and fears. It brings about a calmness and inner peace that ultimately leads to rejoicing once your prayers are answered. You would be amazed by what God can do in your life, as long as it is in accordance to His good will. Asking for a million dollars is foolishness, but asking for Him to deliver you from jail with a contrite heart is not.

Remember that God is an all loving Father who only wants the best for you, and though you may feel "scolded" now, I can assure you that in time, you will feel completely loved and provided for. I am here to tell you that it is possible. God's good Grace has provided me with so much Hope that it amazes me even to this day. I am now back working as a pharmacist and am able to pay my bills independently now, and considering my past, that is a real blessing! But it certainly did not happen overnight. It happened in God's planned timing for me. Could I have achieved this on my own? Absolutely and resolutely not! I say that emphatically because I am able to clearly look back and see how easily I messed things up. It was only by God's help and good Grace that it was restored.

Will you encounter doubters? Most certainly you will. Family or friends may doubt your resolve or ability to stay clean, but you shouldn't concern yourself with that. Don't take it personally. Sometimes our past follows us. It's putting your faith in God and trusting Him completely to lead you to where you are supposed to be that should be your main concern. When you do that, everything else will fall into place.

Even if something does not go the way you were expecting it to, trust that God has a better plan in store for you. Perhaps you applied for a new job and were not hired, do not fret over it. Perhaps your application for an apartment was turned down. It just means that God has someplace better for you to work and live. Trust in Him and His timing and see how good He is. And no matter how bad your past life may have been, it will all seem like a distant memory to you. Trusting in God's timing always turns into a blessing and joy.

Living As God Intended

"I assure you, anyone who obeys my teaching will never die!" John 8:51

Are you longing to be somewhere else, anywhere but where you are now? You know you were meant for something better, but circumstances have led you to a bad place now. Perhaps you are advertising yourself online to help support your drug habit, lying down with different men throughout the day to make money. Perhaps you are stealing from a family member or an employer. Have you bought drugs before purchasing food for your child? Perhaps you have lost custody of your child because of your drug habit. Or maybe you are reading this inside a jail cell, wondering what you can do to get out. Well I am here to tell you that it is never too late to change. God loves each and every one of us. He wants the brokenhearted to call out to Him, for it says so in the Bible. In my moment of desperation, I prayed that God would deliver me from my situation, and He did!

God wants better things for us, if we would just trust Him to provide those things for us. We have but to ask, it's just that simple. Trust God to bring you up out of that dark place you are in now, and be amazed by what is possible through Him. It may be difficult for you to imagine right now. To imagine yourself not using drugs, or walking away from that jail, or getting custody of your child back, but if you take that first step and pray for His mercy and forgiveness, then that impossible becomes real.

"How does God intend me to live?" you may ask. If I may, I would like to bring us back into the Old Testament of the Bible for a minute. When Moses led the Jewish people out of Egypt and towards the Promised Land, they built a portable temple so that God's presence could always be with them. This temple traveled with the people, but only the Levites, a priestly clan of the Jewish population, were able to tend to and carry it. And of the Levites, only the high priest was able to enter it to offer sacrifices to God to atone for the people's sins, making them acceptable to God again.

Eventually the people settled into Israel, and King Solomon built a magnificent temple where the people could come to worship God. God promised to protect them as long as they worshiped only Him. It was only after the people started worshiping other gods and drifted deeper and deeper into sin that the people of Israel were scattered to other nations and the temple was destroyed.

Now that we have Jesus as the perfect sacrifice to wash away all of our sins, we ought to think of our bodies as God's temple. Injecting ourselves with addicting drugs will only serve to destroy that temple. Prostituting ourselves will only prevent God's Spirit from residing within us. Worshiping other gods, so to speak, will only serve to separate us from Him. Our body is God's temple, and we should treat it as such. By praying to the High Priest, Jesus, and earnestly asking Him to forgive our sins, we have taken that first step to restoring ourselves to God, and thereby restoring His temple.

When you stop polluting your body with drugs, it makes it possible for God's Spirit to reside within you. Once the Jews repented and cried out for God's help, they were able to return to Israel and rebuild the temple. This didn't happen without some struggles and difficulties, but the impossible became possible for them. And it is possible for you too. No matter what obstacle you are facing, with God's help, you too can be delivered and restored.

"But what happens next?" you may ask. "I've prayed for forgiveness and asked for help. What do I do now?" Be patient and see, have faith. It took three long and tiresome days before He made it possible for me to bail out of jail, but it happened. It may take considerably longer than that for the one reading this in jail now, but never give up hope. With God anything is possible. Watch and see Him open the doors of opportunity for you as He did for me. Remember to turn away from the things that caused you to sin. For the addict, that may require time away in a rehab center, but take heart and look at that as a path towards your new life, living as God intended you to. For the mother seeking custody of her child again, you may have to prove to the court that you are a fit mother now. Maintaining your sobriety is going to be a requirement, so remember to treat your body as God's temple and get yourself clean. For the one in jail, you may be required to do a long period of probation which also requires random drug testing, but does that not beat sitting inside a jail cell?

Sometimes it takes a person to hit a rock bottom before they realize just how blessed they are. Giving thanks to God for His deliverance is far better than traveling that dreary path of drug use and all of its downfalls. By stopping your drug use, it changes you and reflects in your life, so much so that people familiar with you can easily see the difference. Family members will want to see you again. You will once again gain the trust of employers and pay bills, providing for yourself and your family. You can offer a safe and stable home environment for your children. All of these things and more are possible with God's help. Won't you come and taste the living waters of God's Spirit and Blessings?